Can You Find It?

Can You Find It?

Judith Cressy

The Metropolitan Museum of Art

Harry N. Abrams, Inc., Publishers

Published in 2002 by The Metropolitan Museum of Art, New York, and Harry N. Abrams, Incorporated, New York
Copyright © 2002 by The Metropolitan Museum of Art

First Edition
Printed in Hong Kong
11 10 09 08 07 06 05 04 03   5 4 3

Produced by the Department of Special Publications, The Metropolitan Museum of Art.
All photography by The Metropolitan Museum of Art Photograph Studio.

Designed by Miriam Berman, with Sophia Stavropoulos

Visit the Museum's Web site: www.metmuseum.org

Library of Congress Cataloging-in-Publication Data
Can you find it?
        p. cm.
        Summary: Presents a diverse collection of well-known paintings which show how,
through the centuries, artists have hidden small details to be discovered by curious eyes.
        ISBN 1-58839-053-5 (MMA).—ISBN 0-8109-3279-2 (Abrams)
        1. Painting—Appreciation—Juvenile literature. [1. Painting. 2. Art appreciation.] I. Harry N. Abrams, Inc.
ND1146.C357   2002   2002018358
759—dc21

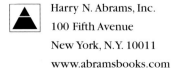

Harry N. Abrams, Inc.
100 Fifth Avenue
New York, N.Y. 10011
www.abramsbooks.com

Abrams is a subsidiary of
LA MARTINIÈRE
GROUPE

In this painting of
a refreshment stand
can you find

1

traffic light

1

woman in blue

3

arrows

1

flight of stairs

2

wreaths

2

pinky rings

&

the word "drink"

&

the word "push" twice

Sweets (detail)
Randall Deihl, American, born 1946
Oil on Masonite

The next time you go to a museum, play the *Can You Find It?* game. You'll need a partner. Together, stand in front of a painting. One of you should find the details and say, "I see a man who looks like a rock," and the other should look for the man who looks like a rock—or whatever detail it is—until it's found. When you move on to the next painting, switch roles. You will soon discover that the closer you look at paintings, the more there is to see.

After hours of playing *Can You Find It?* at The Metropolitan Museum of Art, we have selected nineteen paintings, packed with fascinating details, that produce an exciting book full of art "discoveries." Our final choices span a variety of periods, cultures, and styles, just like the collections at the Museum.

Fifteenth-century Netherlandish painting, with its emphasis on clarity, is a perfect choice. Nineteenth-century American folk art, too, is easy to draw from, since many self-taught painters seemed intent on including every brick, cobblestone, and shop sign in sight. Ancient Egyptian tomb paintings are full of intriguing details, and so are Indian and Chinese images. But, alas, there are no French Impressionist paintings here, because the details tend to dissolve into brushstrokes when you get up close.

When you visit a museum, you can play *Can You Find It?* with any painting, whether it contains just one great detail or twenty. The fun is in the exciting *aha!* of discovery. We hope this book will inspire many excited gasps as you uncover the treasures of art.

— Judith Cressy

In this painting of
a small town
can you find

1

bridge

1

man in a top hat

9

horse-drawn vehicles

1

carriage
without a horse

1

horse
without a carriage

1

water pump

1

load of hay

1

barn with open doors

View of Poestenkill, New York (detail)
Joseph H. Hidley, American, 1830–1872
Oil on wood

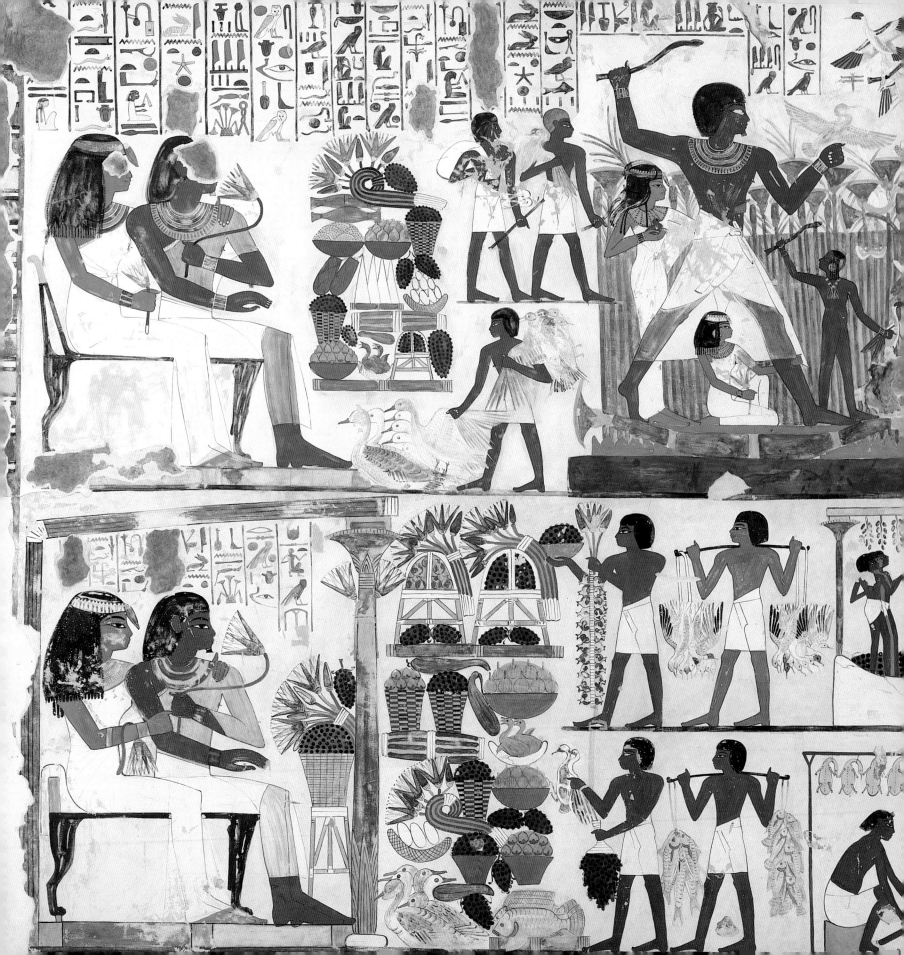

In this painting from
ancient Egypt
can you find

5
butterflies

4
zucchini

2
boats

7
woven baskets

2
bowls of grapes

2
owls with yellow wings

18
eggs

1
woman holding a duckling

Scenes from the Tomb of Nakht (detail)
Unknown artist
Egyptian, Thebes, Sheikh abd Qurna, Dynasty 18, circa 1425 B.C.
Tempera on paper facsimile by Norman de Garis Davies

In this painting of
people dancing
can you find

2

brass horns

3

tall hats

2

violins

5

open fans

1

walking stick

1

steaming cup

1

small pitcher

5

blue bows

A Dance in the Country
Giovanni Domenico Tiepolo, Italian, Venice, 1727–1804
Oil on canvas

In this painting of
**harvesters
in a wheat field**
can you find

2

flying birds

4

bowls

2

baskets

3

cows

1

pitchfork

4

jugs

1

ladder

&

some apples

The Harvesters (detail)
Pieter Bruegel the Elder, Netherlandish,
active by 1551–died 1569
Oil on wood

In this painting of
an outdoor feast
can you find

1

fox

4

birds

1

bear throwing a rock

1

man who looks
like a rock

2

leopards

1

donkey

4

bottles

6

beards

The Feast of Sāda
Sultān Muhammad, Iranian, Tabriz,
Safavid period, circa 1522–24
Page from the *Shahnāma*
(Book of Kings) by Firdausī,
colors, ink, silver, and gold on paper

In this painting of
a young prince and his friend
can you find

5

hands

2

coats of arms

1

bridge

2

hats

1

spring of water

1

sun face

1

tiny horse and rider

&

the date 1603 twice

Henry Frederick (1594–1612),
Prince of Wales, and Sir John Harington
(1592–1614)
Robert Peake the Elder, British,
active by 1576–died 1619
Oil on canvas

In this painting of
**a train
at a station**
can you find

2
little white dogs

1
pair of oxen

2
parasols

1
brass bell

1
soldier with a
crutch

1
newspaper

1
pair of antlers

&
the time 9:45

The 9:45 Accommodation
(detail)
Edward Lamson Henry,
American, 1841-1919
Oil on canvas

16

In this painting of
San Francisco
can you find

6

ships

3

palm trees

3

bridges

1

wiggly road

1

tunnel

3

pagodas

1

doughnut-shaped building

&

the number 76 twice

View of San Francisco, Number 2
Peter Saul, American, born 1934
Oil and acrylic on canvas

In this painting of
boats in Venice
can you find

2

barrels

3

halos

2

people
hidden in doorways

3

women
with white head scarves

4

men
with walking sticks

3

domes

1

eight-pointed star

3

statues with wings

Venice: Santa Maria della Salute
Canaletto (Giovanni Antonio Canal),
Italian, Venice, 1697–1768
Oil on canvas

In this painting of
a masquerade ball
can you find

1

chandelier

1

man in a white wig

1

woman with a fan

1

tiara

1

chair in the air

1

sword

1

spearhead

1

man in a turban

Masquerade Ball at the Ritz Hotel, Paris
Raimundo de Madrazo y Garreta,
Spanish, 1841–1920
Oil on canvas

In this painting of
a scene in China
can you find

2

seated men

1

baby

3

green chests

1

man on a roof

1

spotted sack

1

archer drawing his bow

1

yellow bowl

1

fallen man

The Abduction of Wenji (detail)
Unknown artist
Chinese, Ming dynasty, 15th century
Ink, color, and gold on silk

24

In this painting of
an art gallery
can you find

1

pyramid

1

man playing two pipes

1

boy removing a thorn
from his foot

1

open book

2

vases of flowers

1

baby

1

dog

3

men on a roof

Ancient Rome (detail)
Giovanni Paolo Pannini, Italian, Rome, 1691–1765
Oil on canvas

In this
painting of
**young
King Louis XV**
can you find

3

hands

1

column

2

buckles

1

crown

1

brooch

8

tassels

3

bunches of lace

1

white bird

Louis XV (1710–1774) as a Child
Hyacinthe Rigaud, French, 1659–1743
Oil on canvas

In this painting of **a couple buying a wedding ring** can you find

1

heart

5

people

4

jeweled brooches

1

arched doorway

2

nails

3

silver coins

1

brown-and-white bird

1

golden bird

A Goldsmith in His Shop, Possibly Saint Eligius
Petrus Christus, Netherlandish, active by 1444–died 1475/76
Oil on wood

In this painting of
**a regiment
on review**
can you find

1

baby in a long white dress

7

blue parasols

1
red flag

1

officer with his hat in his hand

4

red shawls

1

man holding a baby

3

little boys in white pants

2

little girls in pink dresses

**Seventh Regiment on Review,
Washington Square, New York** (detail)
Otto Boetticher, German, circa 1816–1864
Oil on canvas

In this painting of

an Indian king

can you find

4

black tassels

2

umbrellas

4

shields

4

bells

1

man with a bow but no arrows

1

man with a spear

6

black feather plumes

3

men with two necklaces

**King Dasharatha and His Royal Retinue
Proceed to Rama's Wedding**
Perhaps by Devidasa of Nurpur,
Indian, Punjab Hills, (Babu) Jammu, circa 1680–90
Page from the dispersed "Shangri" *Ramayana*,
ink and opaque watercolor on paper

In this painting of
peasants at a party
can you find

3

little dogs

1

bagpipe

3

babies

2

smoking chimneys

6

red caps

6

brown jugs

1

hole in a roof

&

the artist's signature

Peasants Dancing and Feasting (detail)
David Teniers the Younger, Flemish, 1610–1690
Oil on canvas

a refreshment stand pages 2-3

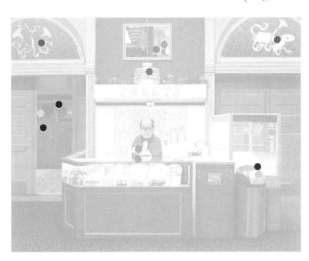

- 1 traffic light
- 1 woman in blue
- 3 arrows
- 1 flight of stairs
- 2 wreaths
- 2 pinky rings
- & the word "drink"
- & the word "push" twice

Sweets, Randall Deihl

The Massachusetts artist Randall Deihl is a realist painter who creates super-detailed scenes of American kitsch that focus on loneliness and alienation. In *Sweets,* the artist depicts the interior of the Academy of Music—once a concert hall, now a movie theater—in Northampton, Massachusetts. Behind the counter, Tommy Bruno, the actual concessionaire at the time the painting was done, stands alone, waiting for business.

Purchase, Frances and Benjamin Benenson Foundation Inc. Gift, 1988   1988.52

a small town pages 6-7

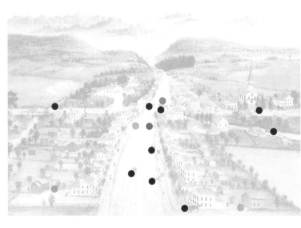

- 1 bridge
- 1 man in a top hat
- 9 horse-drawn vehicles
- 1 carriage without a horse
- 1 horse without a carriage
- 1 water pump
- 1 load of hay
- 1 barn with open doors

View of Poestenkill, New York, Joseph H. Hidley

Joseph Henry Hidley spent most of his life in Poestenkill, New York, a town about eight miles east of Troy. Hidley worked as a housepainter, handyman, artist, and taxidermist. All of his paintings are town views. This one looks down Poestenkill's main street. The Evangelical Lutheran Church is the most imposing building in the painting. Hidley lived next to the church.

Gift of Edgar William and Bernice Chrysler Garbisch, 1963   63.201.5

ancient Egypt pages 8-9

- 5 butterflies
- 4 zucchini
- 2 boats
- 7 woven baskets
- 2 bowls of grapes
- 2 owls with yellow wings
- 18 eggs
- 1 woman holding a duckling

Scenes from the Tomb of Nakht, unknown artist

The wall paintings in Egyptian tombs were intended to provide the spirits of the tomb owner and his family with whatever they needed in the afterlife. In these scenes, Nakht and his family hunt on the marshes; Nakht and his wife Tawi receive offerings of food; and workmen make wine and catch and prepare wild birds.

Rogers Fund, 1915   15.5.19e

people dancing pages 10-11

- 2 brass horns
- 3 tall hats
- 2 violins
- 5 open fans
- 1 walking stick
- 1 steaming cup
- 1 small pitcher
- 5 blue bows

A Dance in the Country, Giovanni Domenico Tiepolo

The son of the great Venetian painter Giovanni Battista Tiepolo, Giovanni Domenico worked alongside his father and his brother in the family business, painting large murals in the homes of the very wealthy, in royal palaces, and in public buildings. He also enjoyed drawing and painting smaller scenes of every-day life, like *A Dance in the Country,* where a troupe of actors in costume are entertaining a party of elegantly dressed Venetians.

Gift of Mr. and Mrs. Charles Wrightsman, 1980   1980.67

harvesters in a wheat field pages 12–13

- 2 flying birds
- 4 bowls
- 2 baskets
- 3 cows
- 1 pitchfork
- 4 jugs
- 1 ladder
- & some apples

The Harvesters, Pieter Bruegel the Elder

This painter is known as Pieter "the Elder" because one of his sons, also named Pieter, was an artist, too. Unlike other important painters of the 1500s, who painted battle scenes, stories from the Bible, and portraits, Pieter Bruegel the Elder looked around him at the Flemish landscape and painted lively scenes of the peasants who farmed it. Here they are gathering wheat, which they would have done each year in late August or early September.

Rogers Fund, 1919   19.164

a young prince and his friend page 15

- 5 hands
- 2 coats of arms
- 1 bridge
- 2 hats
- 1 spring of water
- 1 sun face
- 1 tiny horse and rider
- & the date 1603 twice

Henry Frederick, Prince of Wales, and Sir John Harington,
Robert Peake the Elder

This portrait was made in 1603, when Prince Henry was nine and his father had just become King James I of England. In the painting, Henry and his companion have completed a stag hunt, which was considered the noblest of kingly pastimes. Henry was raised to become the next king, but he died of typhoid fever at the age of eighteen, leaving the throne to his brother, who ruled as Charles I.

Purchase, Joseph Pulitzer Bequest, 1944   44.27

an outdoor feast page 14

- 1 fox
- 4 birds
- 1 bear throwing a rock
- 1 man who looks like a rock
- 2 leopards
- 1 donkey
- 4 bottles
- 6 beards

The Feast of Sāda,
Sultān Muhammad

Written in the tenth century by the Iranian poet Firdausī, the *Shahnāma,* or *Book of Kings,* is a history complete with handsome champions, beautiful maidens, treacherous demons, and monarchs—both good and wicked. In this illustration from the book, the ruler Hushang has recognized fire as a divine gift. He has gathered his courtiers to tell them about the potential of fire, and to celebrate the feast that would become known as Sāda.

Gift of Arthur A. Houghton Jr., 1970   1970.301.2

a train at a station pages 16–17

- 2 little white dogs
- 1 pair of oxen
- 2 parasols
- 1 brass bell
- 1 soldier with a crutch
- 1 newspaper
- 1 pair of antlers
- & the time 9:45

The 9:45 Accommodation, Edward Lamson Henry

Born in Charleston, South Carolina, Henry was orphaned at an early age, and was brought to live with cousins in New York in 1848. After training as an artist, he became interested in transportation and painted a number of pictures of carriages, horses, wagons, ships, and trains. *The 9:45 Accommodation* was painted in 1867 for John Taylor Johnston, president of the New Jersey Central Railroad and first president of The Metropolitan Museum of Art.

Bequest of Moses Tanenbaum, 1937   39.47.1

San Francisco pages 18–19

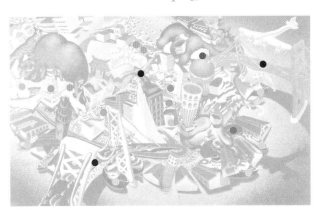

- 6 ships
- 3 palm trees
- 3 bridges
- 1 wiggly road
- 1 tunnel
- 3 pagodas
- 1 doughnut-shaped building
- & the number 76 twice

View of San Francisco, Number 2, Peter Saul

Born in San Francisco, Peter Saul now lives and works in New York. Bright colors and a cartoonlike style have been part of his work throughout his long career. In Saul's paintings, everything seems to be alive and moving. Viewed from above, San Francisco gets its liveliness from the flow of energy across the bridges and the rubbery quality of boats and buildings bending and colliding.

Arthur Hoppock Hearn Fund, 1988   1988.312

a masquerade ball pages 22–23

- 1 chandelier
- 1 man in a white wig
- 1 woman with a fan
- 1 tiara
- 1 chair in the air
- 1 sword
- 1 spearhead
- 1 man in a turban

Masquerade Ball at the Ritz Hotel, Paris, Raimundo de Madrazo y Garreta

Members of Raimundo de Madrazo y Garreta's family were among the most important painters in nineteenth-century Spain. Raimundo, who inherited the family talent, left Spain to work in Paris and New York. He specialized in portraits of women and was noted for his intimate scenes of high society.

Bequest of Emma T. Gary, 1934   37.20.3

boats in Venice pages 20–21

- 2 barrels
- 3 halos
- 2 people hidden in doorways
- 3 women with white head scarves
- 4 men with walking sticks
- 3 domes
- 1 eight-pointed star
- 3 statues with wings

Venice: Santa Maria della Salute, Canaletto (Giovanni Antonio Canal)

During the more than forty-five years of Canaletto's career, he was known for his view paintings. In the 1700s, scenic views of cities, harbors, and antique architecture were extremely popular. Canaletto's main subject was his native Venice, Italy, one of the most picturesque cities in the world. He was especially interested in capturing the effects of sunlight and shadow in his paintings. The results were dramatic.

Purchase, George T. Delacorte Jr. Gift, 1959   59.38

a scene in China pages 24–25

- 2 seated men
- 1 baby
- 3 green chests
- 1 man on a roof
- 1 spotted sack
- 1 archer drawing his bow
- 1 yellow bowl
- 1 fallen man

The Abduction of Wenji, unknown artist

This is a detail from a Chinese scroll that tells a story called Eighteen Songs of a Nomad Flute. The story begins in about the year 195, when Lady Wenji was abducted from her father's home. Taken to Inner Mongolia, she was forced to marry the chief of a nomad tribe. Many years passed before a ransom mission found her. Lady Wenji then faced a painful choice: to remain with her husband and children in a land that she despised, or to return to her own people in China. She returned to China.

Ex. coll.: C. C. Wang Family, Gift of The Dillon Fund, 1973   1973.120.3

an art gallery page 26-27

- 1 pyramid
- 1 man playing two pipes
- 1 boy removing a thorn from his foot
- 1 open book
- 2 vases of flowers
- 1 baby
- 1 dog
- 3 men on a roof

Ancient Rome, Giovanni Paolo Pannini

Views of famous monuments were popular with European art collectors of the 1700s and often served the same purpose that travel souvenirs do today. Pannini was among the best-known view painters of his time, and the work reproduced here is one of his most brilliant inventions: All of the tiny framed images are actual views of Rome. The comte de Stainville, who commissioned the painting, stands at its center with his walking stick.

Gwynne Andrews Fund, 1951   52.63.1

a couple buying a wedding ring
page 29

- 1 heart
- 5 people
- 4 jeweled brooches
- 1 arched doorway
- 2 nails
- 3 silver coins
- 1 brown-and-white bird
- 1 golden bird

A Goldsmith in His Shop, Possibly Saint Eligius,
Petrus Christus

A master painter of the 1400s, Petrus Christus worked in the city of Bruges, Belgium. In this painting, one of his most famous, Christus shows a young couple in a goldsmith's shop, picking out their wedding rings. It is thought that the painting might have been commissioned by a goldsmiths' guild to advertise its services. Saint Eligius is the patron saint of goldsmiths and metalworkers.

Robert Lehman Collection, 1975   1975.1.110

young King Louis XV page 28

- 3 hands
- 1 column
- 2 buckles
- 1 crown
- 1 brooch
- 8 tassels
- 3 bunches of lace
- 1 white bird

Louis XV (1710–1774) as a Child,
Hyacinthe Rigaud

This fine portrait of Louis XV, one of many versions, was painted when he was only five and had just become king of France. Others ruled for him until Louis's actual coronation, which took place when he was thirteen.

Portraits were Hyacinthe Rigaud's specialty; he painted an average of thirty-five of them a year for sixty-two years, working mainly at the French royal court.

Purchase, Bequest of Mary Wetmore Shively, in memory of her husband,
Henry L. Shively M.D., 1960   60.6

a regiment on review pages 30-31

- 1 baby in a long white dress
- 7 blue parasols
- 1 red flag
- 1 officer with his hat in his hand
- 4 red shawls
- 1 man holding a baby
- 3 little boys in white pants
- 2 little girls in pink dresses

Seventh Regiment on Review, Washington Square, New York,
Otto Boetticher

Born in Germany, Otto Boetticher came to America in about 1850 and worked as a lithographer in New York. It is for Boetticher's detailed paintings and prints of military life that he is remembered today. He knew his subject well: During the Civil War, he was an officer of the Sixty-eighth New York Volunteer Regiment and was made lieutenant colonel in 1865.

The Edward W. C. Arnold Collection of New York Prints, Maps, and Pictures,
Bequest of Edward W. C. Arnold, 1954   54.90.29

an Indian king pages 32-33

- 4 black tassels
- 2 umbrellas
- 4 shields
- 4 bells
- 1 man with a bow but no arrows
- 1 man with a spear
- 6 black feather plumes
- 3 men with two necklaces

King Dasharatha and His Royal Retinue Proceed to Rama's Wedding,
perhaps by Devidasa of Nurpur

From the sixteenth through the nineteenth century, artists in Northern and Central India produced paintings for the pleasure of their rulers and their royal circles. Many of the paintings done for the Hindu courts were illustrations of popular stories from religious texts. This painting of a colorful and tumultuous procession is an illustration from the *Ramayana, The Story of King Rama.*

Purchase, The Dillon Fund, Evelyn Kranes Kossak, and Anonymous Gifts, 1994   1994.310

peasants at a party pages 34-35

- 3 little dogs
- 1 bagpipe
- 3 babies
- 2 smoking chimneys
- 6 red caps
- 6 brown jugs
- 1 hole in a roof
- & the artist's signature

Peasants Dancing and Feasting, David Teniers the Younger

Teniers's father and son, David I and David III, were also painters, and David II ("the Younger") married the daughter of another well-known Antwerp artist, Jan Bruegel the Elder. Teniers painted hundreds of pictures, including many scenes of peasants in taverns, in barns, or outside country inns (as here).
His other subjects include biblical stories, landscapes, portraits, and views of collectors' cabinets.

Purchase, 1871   71.99

ancient Egypt back cover

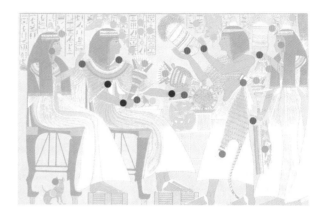

- 2 cats
- 6 lotus blossoms
- 3 eye amulets
- 3 earrings
- 8 thumbs
- 1 grapevine
- 2 leopard paws
- 10 ∧∧∧∧ signs

Ipuy and His Wife Duam-meres Receiving Offerings from Their Children,
unknown artist

Ipuy was a sculptor during the reign of Ramesses II, one of Egypt's best-known kings. He and his family lived in Deir el-Medina, a village of artists who built and decorated the royal tombs. Ipuy's tomb was probably decorated by one of his colleagues. Since Egyptian artists didn't sign their work, the creators of almost all ancient Egyptian art are anonymous.

Rogers Fund, 1930   30.4.114